Patience Agbabi was born in London in 1965 and educated at Oxford and Sussex Universities. Renowned for her live performances, her poems have been broadcast on television and radio all over the world. Her work has also appeared on the London Underground and human skin. She has lectured in Creative Writing at several UK universities including Greenwich, Cardiff and Kent. In 2004 she was nominated one of the UK's Next Generation Poets. *Bloodshot Monochrome* is her third poetry collection. She lives in Kent with her partner and two children.

Also by Patience Agbabi

R.A.W.
Transformatrix

BLOODSHOT MONOCHROME

PATIENCE AGBABI

CANONGATE

Edinburgh · London

First published in Great Britain in 2008 by
Canongate Books Ltd, 14 High Street,
Edinburgh EH1 1TE

The TS Eliot quote on p. 37 is from 'Philip Massinger', *Selected Prose of TS Eliot*, ed. Frank Kermode (Faber and Faber Ltd). Reproduced with permission.

British Library Cataloguing-in-Publication Data
A catalogue record for this book is available on
request from the British Library

ISBN 978 1 84767 153 0

Typeset by Palimpsest Book Production Ltd, Grangemouth,
Stirlingshire

www.canongate.tv

ACKNOWLEDGEMENTS

I would like to thank the following journals, in which poems for this collection have appeared in some form: *Atlas, BBC Poetry Proms Pamphlet,* www.blinking-eye.co.uk, www.madhattersreview.com/issue8/england_index.shtml, *Poetry Review, Pratik, The Red Wheelbarrow, Trespass, Vogue.*

Some poems have also appeared in the following anthologies: *Here to Eternity* (Faber & Faber), *New Writing 12* (Picador), *Poems on the Underground* (Cassell), *POP Anthology* (New Departures), *Velocity* (Apples & Snakes).

'The London Eye' was a Poem on the Underground. It was originally commissioned for *Earth Has Not Any Thing To Shew More Fair,* ed. Peter Oswald and Alice Oswald and Robert Woof (Shakespeare's Globe & The Wordsworth Trust). The book was a bicentenary celebration of Wordsworth's 'Composed Upon Westminster Bridge, Sept. 3, 1802'. 'Man and Boy' and 'The Siamese Twins' were originally commissioned by BBC Radio 3 for Poetry Proms. 'North(west)ern' was originally commissioned in 2000 by Radio 4 for *The Windrose*, and was made into a short film for BBC Knowledge. 'Osmosis' was commissioned for a Southern Arts postcard celebrating a Year of the Artist Residency at the Schools of Humanities and Healthcare at Oxford Brookes University in 2001. 'There was an old woman who lived in a shoe' was commissioned as part of the Faltered States performance project (2003) by Apples & Snakes and the Science Museum.

Several of these poems appear on the iPoems system hosted on www.57productions.com.

I would also like to thank Jamie Byng, Francis Bickmore and everyone at Canongate for their enthusiasm and commitment to the book; Jeremy Clarke, Kwame Dawes, Matthew Hollis, Steve Tasane, Geoff Allnutt and Patricia Debney for their insightful feedback on the manuscript; Kate Clanchy for reminding me there is creative life after motherhood and Louisa Stevens for keeping me focused; Jennifer Russell, Sue Booth-Forbes and Susan DeBow for helping me kickstart the 'Shots' section at Anam Cara; to Gary Bagot for giving me the plot for 'Yore Just My Type' and Adeola Agbebiyi for the song title 'Slow-Burning Fuse' in 'Josephine Baker Finds Herself'; Thabitha Khumalo for alerting me to the issues of women in Zimbabwe for 'What's Black and White and Red All Over?'; Peter Abbs, Ros Barber and all those on the MA at Sussex for their invaluable feedback on 'Vicious Circle' and the late Carl St Hill for believing in it.

The poet would like to thank the Authors' Foundation and the AHRB for grants enabling me to write and develop as a writer and lecturer.

Finally, special thanks to all the contributors to *Problem Pages*, for their sonnets and their prose. Without their presiding spirits this book would never have been written.

CONTENTS

SHOTS

SEEING RED

1

Black mum parts my continent of head,
with glazed black cotton begins to wind
each division so fiercely my mind
bleeds black. I can't close my eyes in bed.

White mum uses fading navy thread,
the tension less cruel, more kind
but the vision colour-blind
so I see red.

2

I read the instructions for shocking-red dye
(freedom has given me the green light)
yet bury the evidence under a head-tie

like the insight
that I see the world through a red eye
where blood and heart mean more than black and white.

POSTMOD:

a snapshot. Monochrome. A woman
in a '60s rayon suit. A knee-length pencil
skirt and jacket with three-quarter sleeves.
Hot aqua and a mod original.
That shade translates to stylish grey. It's me.
And on the back, someone's scrawled in pencil
Brighton Beach, 1963

for fun because I wasn't even thought of
in 1963. Imagine Rhyl,
'82, where the image was conceived
by someone with good taste, bad handwriting
and lack of a camera. Yet that negative,
in our heads only, was as sharp and real
as the suit so out of fashion it was in.

GREY AREA

We two sip wine outside a Jo'burg café.

Soweto's bloody dangerous, don't go
till it's over she says. I don't respond.

A white man swaggers by with a black
woman who's not his wife, girlfriend or date.

A black man curses her in Xhosa.
                        Click.
                        The white man pulls out a gun and

I'm sitting so close I could lift my hand, touch metal.

Slow motion back
to our car.   No split second.

The beer is ice-cold in Soweto, cold as lead.
Home is a grey area yet safe.

I don't want to go.

SHOOTING 'UFO WOMAN'

Action! Alien with Day-Glo afro
(wig) and eyes (lens) like stained-glass window,
mount silver stairs, float down to earth
(down-escalator Canary Wharf),
make earthling (hardcore dealer) pause en route
to admire strange skin (ogle PVC spacesuit).

Alien would conquer world
from business epicentre, with S-Curl

but the lens regressed to sand, attacked my eye
and blaxploitation sci-fi
turned film noir.
         I left in dark glasses,
in a black cab like Metamorphosis,
each streetlight burning in my vision
how fact (I could be blind for life) shot fiction.

NOT A 9/11 POEM

No, postmen don't get postman's block.
They may deliver the wrong letters
but are never stuck for a line break
or line. If you think writers,

poets are lazy, give them enough real work
to sweat out their poems, a tragedy
like 9/11 and a week
to work on their wordplay

and watch them divide
into poets for spontaneous
overflow and poets for emotions made vivid
months later in the aftermath, the stillness

but since there's still no peace there's still no poem,
no postmortem.

'GANGSTERS'

shot straight into the Top 10 and school
uniform was dead. Ties tapered,
blazers trailed and we all murdered
to look as miserable as Terry Hall
or mad as Jerry Dammers whose smile
was a few keys short of a keyboard.
We didn't get the 2-tone metaphor;
know the rankin' rude bwoy model
was Peter Tosh; that the Wailers
preached 'Simmer Down' in '63 to stop
rough an' tough on the dancefloor,
but for ska to rule the airwaves
Sometime people got roughed up.
We knew what it meant, 'music to die for'.

THE LONDON EYE

Through my gold-tinted Gucci sunglasses,
the sightseers. Big Ben's quarter chime
strikes the convoy of number 12 buses
that bleeds into the city's monochrome.

Through somebody's zoom lens, me shouting
to you, *Hello! . . . on . . . bridge . . . 'minster!*
The aerial view postcard, the man writing
squat words like black cabs in rush hour.

The South Bank buzzes with a rising treble.
You kiss my cheek, formal as a blind date.
We enter Cupid's capsule, a thought bubble
where I think, 'Space age!', you think, 'She was late.'

Big Ben strikes six. My SKIN .Beat™ blinks, replies
18·02. We're moving anticlockwise.

ON TURNING ON THE TV TO CATCH,
BY CHANCE, SOME QUAVERING BARS
OF 'SUMMERTIME', THAT VOICE, PITCH,
BLACK AS A SEMIBREVE, SCARS
ON THE FACE FILLING THE BLANK SCREEN,
THE BLURRED BLACK-AND-WHITE IMAGE
OF JANIS JOPLIN'S SYNAESTHETIC SCREAM,
ALL HIPPY HAIR AND CLASS A VINTAGE;
MY REACTION MIRRORING MAMA CASS
AT MONTEREY WATCHING 'BALL AND CHAIN'
CLIMB TO A CLIMAX; THE HEAVY BASS,
THEN JANIS TAKING IT DEEP DOWN DOWN –
TO THE BLUES, THE DEEP SOUTH, THE NEXT FIX
OF ROCK 'N' ROLL AND HEROIN AND SEX.

Wow!

COMEDOWN

The mind is its own place, and in itself
Can make a heav'n of hell, a hell of heav'n.
                    Milton, *Paradise Lost*

It wasn't the rent boy we met in Heaven
who looked fifteen and called us dollies,
with his social worker as an accessory
I thought was his boyfriend, leading us up
to the party full of lacklustre women
in tight polyester, and upstairs, not
the Skin with the spider's web tattoo
for a face, that bled red light in my skull;
nor the ugly man who said *Full of fucking*
spades and half-castes as soon as we entered
whom I misheard, the social worker
doing his damnedest to sugar the pill:
it was taking a drug that made us innocent
enough to leave Heaven and end up in Hell.

FOREIGN EXCHANGE

In Hamburg, me and Anna, who is German,
and a man across the street attacks us, spitting
his violence; the air is cold, and bitter
faces gather like rainclouds, like an omen
and my gentle friend counter-attacks but later
refuses to translate and that's the killer,
her silence, like a shroud; I feel the colour
rage in my cheeks for lack of that translation

reminding me of school, that French exchange,
a simple sentence, *Parce qu'elle est noire*,
delivered at such speed and with such hatred
it stung me: to encounter so much rage;
more, for being judged solely by colour;
but most, the fact it had to be translated.

NORTH(WEST)ERN

I was twelve, as in the twelve-bar blues, sick
for the Southeast, marooned on the North Wales coast.
A crotchet, my tongue craving the music
of Welsh, Scouse or Manc. Entering the outpost
of Colwyn Bay pier, midsummer, noon,
nightclub for those of us with the deep ache
of adolescence, when I heard that tune,
named it in one. Soul. My heart was break

dancing on the road to Wigan Casino,
Northern Soul Mecca where transatlantic bass
beat blacker than blue in glittering mono.

Then back, via Southport, Rhyl, to the time, place,
I bit the Big Apple. Black, impatient, young.
A string of pips exploding on my tongue.

SOL

After I huffed, puffed, pushed you into the pool
of light and blood on the crushed white sheet
you screamed like an abattoir, like shit,
breaking the day to smithereens until
they swaddled you, our son, our Sol:
you were light, light-skinned, skinny, sugar-sweet,
hair iridescent with blood, eyes bloodshot
but they said they would heal

and they did. Home, we keep you in the shade
in a basket bed where we watch you grow
golden, golden brown, your eyes indigo
to bronze, stare and stare at the ladybird
with a rattle for a heart. All you know
is mum and dad, is black and white, and red.

MONOLOGUES

THE SIAMESE TWINS

And she arose at midnight and took my [child] from beside me,
while thine handmaid slept, and laid it in her bosom, and laid
her dead child in my bosom.

1 Kings 3:20

Excuse me. Janie isn't it? I'm Rhea.
I'm deeply sorry. Yes, I knew your mother.
You won't remember me, you were a baby
when we last met. Your mother might have mentioned . . . ?
She didn't? No, 'The Times' obituary.
I thought I should attend, pay my respects,
she was an inspiration to us all.
A tricky act to follow, I imagine.
The service was sublime, so many flowers.
A gin and tonic, thank you. Mother's ruin.
Do you have any children? Yes and no.

I met your mother forty years ago
in hospital. Both of us were expecting,
had both had false alarms. They kept us in.
Her bed was next to mine and soon we gelled
so well they nicknamed us The Siamese Twins.
Your mother smuggled in forbidden foods –
hospitals were like prisons in those days –
and every night we'd have a midnight feast.
She kept me sane. When the pains started
she held my hand until the nurses came.
We both had baby girls on the same day.
The 21st of May, 1960.
Your birthday, dear. I called my baby Sophie.
Your mother couldn't decide between Amanda
and Jane. I said, *She looks like a Jane.*
I felt so thrilled, so overjoyed, I cried.

Twenty-four hours later, Sophie died.
I laid on her, they said. I started rocking.
It took three doctors and a sedative
to separate me from her. Yes, I'm fine,
thank you. I can't remember much about
the funeral. Except I couldn't cry.
So many flowers. All I can remember
is being back in hospital, visiting
your mother there and finding her asleep.
I picked you up, Janie, started walking
down corridors and stairs and corridors.
Nobody stopped me. No one ever does.
You didn't stir until we reached the car
and when you cried, I held you to my breast
and fed you. Janie, don't you understand?
My husband and the doctors and now you.
I should have been your mother, it was fate
that Sophie died. You were identical,
one egg split into two. They locked me up
until I was too old to bear more children.
They wouldn't let you visit me. Each week
I read about your mother in the papers
and sometimes you. Nobody knows I'm here.
Don't cry, Janie, I'm your mother now.
I knew that one day we'd be reunited
like this. A mother needs a daughter, dear.
All I want is half your heart to know
I love you, Jane. God's gracious gift, don't go.

EAT ME

When I hit thirty, he brought me a cake,
three layers of icing, home-made,
a candle for each stone in weight.

The icing was white but the letters were pink,
they said, *EAT ME*. And I ate, did
what I was told. Didn't even taste it.

Then he asked me to get up and walk
round the bed so he could watch my broad
belly wobble, hips judder like a juggernaut.

The bigger the better, he'd say, *I like*
big girls, soft girls, girls I can burrow inside
with multiple chins, masses of cellulite.

I was his Jacuzzi. But he was my cook,
my only pleasure the rush of fast food,
his pleasure, to watch me swell like forbidden fruit.

His breadfruit. His desert island after shipwreck.
Or a beached whale on a king-size bed
craving a wave. I was a tidal wave of flesh

too fat to leave, too fat to buy a pint of full-fat milk,
too fat to use fat as an emotional shield,
too fat to be called chubby, cuddly, big-built.

The day I hit thirty-nine, I allowed him to stroke
my globe of a cheek. His flesh, my flesh flowed.
He said, *Open wide*, poured olive oil down my throat.

Soon you'll be forty . . . he whispered, and how
could I not roll over on top. I rolled and he drowned
in my flesh. I drowned his dying sentence out.

I left him there for six hours that felt like a week.
His mouth slightly open, his eyes bulging with greed.
There was nothing else left in the house to eat.

SKINS

It's not like you don't turn me on.
Every time you walked past
I thought, *She's fit.*
Come-to-bed eyes.
We both want to
feel my skin

against your skin.
It's not like you're on
or I'm changing into
a woman. It's my past.
Look into my eyes.
I just wanted to fit

in. A misfit.
Mixed-race but light-skinned,
brown hair, blue eyes,
bootboy with a hard-on.
I passed.
I had to.

Then I got this tattoo.
I did it in a fit
of rage. It soon passed.
You want to read my skin?
Whatever turns you on.
I closed my eyes

and put my soul on ice,
denied a black dad, too
terrified to let on.
I wore the outfit,
marched with the skins.
I don't like to talk about the past,

I hate my past.
My big lie reflected in their eyes,
their hatred in my skin.
With this tattoo
I'm a walking Photofit.
That's why I keep my clothes on.

It's past midnight. I'll call a cab if you want me to.
But your eyes know how to fit
a condom like a second skin. Come on . . .

YORE JUST MY TYPE

You can't find a good gay shag unless you pay for it
in airmiles. Berlin. All you get is shit
in your own backyard. Take this lad I met on Gaydar.
Said I was just what he wanted. Good sex, car,
roast dinner on Sunday and all that crap. I believed him.
Ten years younger, spent his life in the gym.
Horny as fuck, his photo. Better in the flesh, he said.
I swallowed it all. Best thing since sliced bread
and I knew where mine was best buttered. Sends me a text:
Yore just my TYPE. I promis more than good SEX.
Still on my phone. I know, but I'm a romantic.
I keep them all. Three days and nights, ten arselick
messages saying how much he loves me and crap.
Problem is, he's near Swansea, not on the map,
and I'm Manchester but he says he's bought a train
ticket for next weekend. I got plans but I rearrange.

Saturday morning he rings to say sorry, got toothache,
has to see emergency dentist. *But it's heartache*
he says *hurts most. I'm gagging to meet you.*
I'm gutted but believe him. We set our rendezvous
for a month's time. I have a few shags but my date's
on my mind. A month to the day my phone vibrates.

It's me he says *you're never gonna believe this . . .*
but of course I do, I'm romantic *but I've got this abscess
on my leg . . .* You see, I've fallen in love so the only bells
ringing in my head are our wedding vowels.
Our third date's set. I fly to Berlin for a shag
with Helmut who used to work in the Reichstag
and wants me to live with him but all I can think of
is some village near Swansea. You see, I've fallen in love
with a lad I never met. And I never meet the wanker!

Rings up the morning he's meant to arrive in Manchester,
says he's leaving for coach station 'cos trains are fucked
at the weekend and I believe him. Just my luck
to fall for a lump of shit. That evening, lover
boy rings to say he's in hospital, got run over
by the Manchester coach, could we make another date?

I'm not a vengeful person but I got this mate
knows a lad, horny, tattooed to fuck, inside
for GBH, doesn't mind his photo being used online.
So I make up this false page on Gaydar and hit on
Swansea: *You're just my type. I'm staying at The Hilton,*
Cardiff . . . crap about champagne and coke.
Swansea replies, *I'll be there in an hour*. The joke
is, he went 'cos the next day he mails a message
asking what went wrong, he must be the village
idiot forgetting to pack his phone and is it too late
for me to text him to make another date?
I do. This is what it says: *FUCK YOU!*

JOSEPHINE BAKER FINDS HERSELF

She picked me up
like a slow-burning fuse. I was down
that girls' club used to run in Brixton,
on acid for fuel. Lipstick lesbians,
techno so hardcore it's spewing out Audis.
She samples my heartbeat and mixes it with
vodka on the rocks. I'm her light-skinned, negative,
twenty-something, short black wavy-bobbed diva.
She purrs *La Garçonne, fancy a drink?* I say
Yes. She's crossing the Star Bar like it's a catwalk. So sleek!
A string of pearls, her flapper dress
studded with low-cut diamonds
through my skin, straight to my heart.
Twenties chic! She works
me up and down. I worship
the way she looks.

The way she looks
me up and down. I worship
twenties chic. She works
through my skin, straight to my heart
studded with low-cut diamonds.
A string of pearls her flapper dress.
Yes! She's crossing the Star Bar like it's a catwalk so sleek
she purrs, la garçonne! *Fancy a drink?* I say.
Twenty-something, short, Black, wavy-bobbed diva:
Vodka on the rocks, I'm her light-skinned negative.
She samples my heartbeat and mixes it with
techno so hardcore it's spewing out Audis
on acid for fuel. *Lipstick Lesbians*,
that girls' club used to run in Brixton
like a slow-burning fuse. I was down.
She picked me up.

HEADS

She was, pray God forgive me, worse than plain.
When I commissioned Holbein, he was paid
to beautify her face with paint. The king
pledged marriage to the portrait, Anne of Cleves.
A Protestant exchange. The date was set,
the table laid, the marriage consecrated.

The wedding feast was tainted, Anne being absent.
Henry, in liquor, claimed the wine was sour.
Addressed the hogshead centrepiece, *M'lady,*
which for my Catholic rivals caused much mirth.
Cromwell, he said, *you mate me with a mare*
I will not mount. Then told the joke about
the virgin executioner unable
to sunder maidenhood nor maiden head.
Roared at his royal wit. Then looked at me.

My fate was set. For Anne Boleyn he hired
the best from France: for me, a beardless boy.
Be not afraid, I said, *pray, take this gift.*
'Tis all I have. Both of our hands were shaking.
I prayed aloud. The crowd, an army shrieking
Traitor! Its face degenerate with hatred.

MAN AND BOY

And Abraham stretched forth his hand,
and took the knife to slay his son.
                                        Genesis 22:10

Open the blind, son. Wide. I'm not dead yet.
Did you hear the hail? Like it was deep frying.
Your mother says forked and sheet lightning
at the same time spells trouble. I know she is.
What's it like, the sky? Blue-grey? Grey-blue?
I wish I could see it too. Like surround
sound with the ghost of a picture.
What's the use? I'm dying. Give me your hand.
Hairy from day one, you were. Born old.
We knew your mother was expecting twins,
expected one of each. Your brother Jacob
followed, gripping your heel, a born tackler.
He takes after your mother. Never trust
a woman. He intends to run the business,
but you were first. There's something I must tell you . . .
I've so few pleasures left. Will you prepare it?
It's OK. Use the Volvo. I'm not going
anywhere, am I? Son, I know you do.

Who is it? Son, is that you? Back so soon?
Come off it. Do you take me for senile?
I've taken leave of one of my senses
not five. Come a bit closer. I don't bite.
You smell, feel like my eldest son yet sound
like Jacob. Is this some kind of a joke?
Forgive me, son. Must be the side effects,
it isn't age that kills you, it's the drugs.
You know there's too much pepper in this soup.
OK. I've kept it buried long enough.
Do something for me first, though. Lock the door
and if your brother knocks, don't answer it.

No one knows this. Not even your mother.
I wish you'd known your grandfather. We're all
cut from the same plain cloth. Identical.
I was an only child, my father and I
did everything together, man and boy.
I'd just turned twelve. My father woke me early,
We're going for a drive. There were two men
I didn't know, the one on the back seat
beside me had black hair, a nervous twitch.
The car smelt of sweat and burning leather.
The journey took forever. No one spoke.
The next thing I remember is the office.
A huge black director's chair, a table,
a telephone, the décor was old-fashioned
but classy. Me, my father, no one else.
Sit down, son. I've never felt so small.
And then he did the thing that shocked me more
than anything that happened since. He tied me.
Tied me to the chair. No. I didn't.
He was my father and his word was law.
He pressed a gun hard up against my head,
my inner eye. Twelve years flashed in a second.
Then the explosion of the phone ringing.
It rang eight times before he answered it.
He didn't speak. Just put down the receiver
and fired the gun towards the candelabra.
We never talked about it. In the car
on the way home, I noticed his grey hairs
for the first time. I never blamed him for it,
I understood. He always kept his word.
He would have fired that shot. He knew I knew.

Bless you son, I'm fine. I need to sleep.
Wake me in three hours' time. I'll drink to that.

Who is it? Who? I'm far too old for this.
If you are who you say you are, then who
the hell sat on my bed, shared my secret?
I've lived too long. He should have pulled the trigger.
Where are my tablets? I'm a dead man.
I have two sons . . . forked and sheet lightning . . .
first come, first served. The sins of the father . . .
Forgive me, son. He let it ring eight times.
I'm sorry, I'm too weak now. Ask your brother.
There's too much salt, I have no appetite.
He went grey overnight. Where are my tablets?
What time is it? Where am I? Who are you?
I only have one son, never had two.

PROBLEM PAGES

CONTRIBUTORS

In Joy and Woe, Henry Howard, Earl of Surrey, ?1517–1547
Two Loves I Have, William Shakespeare, 1564–1616
A Crowne of Sonnets, Lady Mary Wroth, 1586/7–1651/2/3
My Light Is Spent, John Milton, 1608–1674
Queen of Shadows, Charlotte Smith, 1749–1806
Scorn Not the Sonnet, William Wordsworth, 1770–1850
O for Ten Years . . ., John Keats, 1795–1821
Not Death, but Love, Elizabeth Barrett Browning, 1806–1861
Send My Roots Rain, Gerard Manley Hopkins, 1844–1889
Not Love but Money, Robert Frost, 1874–1963
On 'The White House', Claude McKay, 1889–1948
Babes in the Basement, Edna St Vincent Millay, 1892–1950
Knew White Speech, Gwendolyn Brooks, 1917–2000
From Africa Singing, June Jordan, 1936–2002

IN JOY AND WOE

Dear Patience, I'm the Mont Blanc of blank verse, the Renoir of rhyme. I've invented a hybrid sonnet that retains the Italian elegance yet is more suited to the modern English tongue. Pierced. My little song is more 'abab' than ABBA. I execute sonnets to unobtainable fillies for fun but my most recent 'gg' is GBH. How do I learn to hold my tongue, my sword?

There's a theory that all criminals are thwarted creatives. But that applies to organised crime. Craft your discipline on the page *and* the stage. Reinvent yourself. Court favour with the critics, use your tongue to celebrate song and remember daily what they say about the pen and the sword.

TWO LOVES I HAVE

Dear Patience, I am a poet who writes for the stage and thus typecast a performance poet. Yet my plays are on the GCSE syllabus so my verse will stand the test of time. My sonnet sequence, addressing a white man and black woman, aims to dress old words new. My publishers claim it will confound the reader but I suspect homophobia/racism. Please help!

I empathise. When will people stop categorising and embrace the page-stage, black-white, heterosexual-homosexual continuum? I applaud your literary range! But who is the reader? Seek critical advice and/or ditch your publisher for one who'll take risks. Your solid reputation will help.

A CROWNE OF SONNETS

Dear Patience, Writing is in my blood: my male muse said *Look in thy heart, and write*. My feminist autobiographical prose romance culminating with a sonnet sequence containing a 14-sonnet corona has sparked controversy and libel accusations. No one explores beyond the prose to appreciate my poetic achievement. Now it has been withdrawn from the shelves.

You could publish the sonnet sequence or corona separately. The latter could stand alone *and* fly off the page, the line repetitions enhancing narrative, a multiplicity of meanings, an intricate music. Few women publish coronas: may yours receive due critical attention on and off the shelf.

MY LIGHT IS SPENT

Dear Patience, I am a middle-aged, respected, white, male poet, neoformalist yet reformist, who is losing his sight, and therefore losing sight of his poetic vision, whose ultimate aim is to implant and cherish in all people the seeds of virtue and public civility. Not writing is death but to write in perpetual darkness is also death. And I lack companionship with women.

I wish more poets shared your ambition. Poetry has long been afraid to admit it wants to change the world. Invest in a dictaphone that transcribes. You may begin to compensate with your other five senses, especially your sixth sense, insight, that will rekindle love of writing. And women.

QUEEN OF SHADOWS

Dear Patience, Wife of a gambler and mother of invention, I write to feed my children. My first book was a sonnet sequence conceived whilst in prison for debt. I borrowed from the past masters to add gravitas to my melancholic landscapes, reflecting a life degraded from colour to black-and-white. Critics screamed plagiarism. I disagree. How do I fight my case?

'Immature poets imitate: mature poets steal; bad poets deface what they take, and good poets make it into something better, or at least something different . . . A good poet will usually borrow from authors remote in time or alien in language, or diverse in interest.' T.S. Eliot. I rest your case.

SCORN NOT THE SONNET

Dear Patience, My first collection was a joint venture with a friend to whom my intellect is most indebted. Subsequently, my sister reacquainted me with the sonnets of Milton, which inspire in simplicity and unity of object and aim: but my friend, my most severe critic, an alcoholic and heroin addict, scorns my 'habit' of writing 'such a multitude of small poems'.

Your intellect is equally indebted to your sister. And Milton is a fine model to imbibe and inject. The sonnet's narrow room can open doors, break glass ceilings. But your friend, invaluable to your development up to this point, is the one who needs help, and to learn to mind his own poems.

O FOR TEN YEARS . . .

Dear Patience, My first book was published at 22, followed with a book-length poem. The reviews drew blood, more about my working-class origins than my poetry. I know the work was flawed. All I need is ten years to develop my style and make it as a poet. But family problems causing financial stress are making me ill. How do I transcend my background?

There's a mean unspoken rule you have to be over thirty before you publish. I'm glad you broke it. Critics can be cruel but a bad review is still exposure. Teach Creative Writing part-time and write one day a week minimum. Learn gardening. It can help pay the rent and keep you grounded.

NOT DEATH, BUT LOVE

Dear Patience, I'm a poet who has spent her life an invalid. But the 'mingled yarn' is black and white. I'm mixed blood. At 38, I desired death, found love. I've written a Petrarchan sonnet sequence to my poet husband. The octave of my life was conflict: the sestet is resolution. How do I resolve whether to reveal the sequence to him, whether to publish?

Enter the private/public debate. You wrote the sonnets *to* him. Is there a chequered skeleton in the cupboard? Is his poetic status your bête noire? Ultimately, we only regret what we don't do. Love is strong as death. Reveal them. It should be a joint decision whether and where you publish.

SEND MY ROOTS RAIN

Dear Patience, I'm a priest first and a poet second. I seek inspiration not publication. Blocked and prone to depression, I believe the only antidepressant is writing. I envy prolific fools. My poetry errs on the side of oddness: I'm drawn to design and pattern, have devised my own rhythms and a ten-and-a-half line version of the sonnet. How do I keep writing?

Confront your conflict of interests. You may be a *poet* second but your writing should always come first. The best way to thwart creativity is to demote it. Envy is the enemy of your innovation. Substitute passion. Write daily, even for five minutes and repeat the mantra *Must keep writing.*

NOT LOVE BUT MONEY

Dear Patience, I am on the cutting edge of contemporary craft. The sonnet is the tightest chamber I have made music in, by subverting its form, becoming its master. To make, not scrape, a living as a poet, I seek not the nod from the literati but applause from the masses. Yet I fear I shall one day regret the road I have chosen, with money as the ultimate drive.

Reverse a second. You've found freedom in form: now seek it in metaphor. Your road has more than one lane. Meticulously crafted poetry can appeal to the élite *and* the masses if accessible. Then there's dumbing down and the cult of celebrity. Love form not fame: beware media overdrive.

ON 'THE WHITE HOUSE'

Dear Patience, I'm a Jamaican griot who's published two collections in the UK/US. I challenge racism and classism in classical sonnets in Standard English. My recent anthology submission, *The White House* was retitled *White Houses* by a black editor. It's not white publishing houses we're banned from but the construct of the American dream.

Congratulations for publishing on two continents! The editor was wrong not to consult you, though it was probably done for your protection. Publish it elsewhere under the correct title. And, why not shake some foundations writing classical sonnets in patois? A progressive publisher's dream.

BABES IN THE BASEMENT

Dear Patience, I'm the femme fatale of the
blank page. I smoke hard, drink men under
the table then cage them in an octave and
sestet. I French kiss babes in basement bars.
Barthes predicted his own death: I read from
memory as my life *is* my work. But the shadow
of my cigarette is shrinking. This can't endure.
Do I bore myself to death or burn myself out?

The wild child in me says keep inspiring that
basement smoke if it fuels great art. Poetry with
bite *is* the new rock 'n' roll. The mother in me
says drink lots of water and eat good food. Heed
both. If you want danger, corset your women into
fourteen lines. It's time more sonnets came out.

KNEW WHITE SPEECH

Dear Patience, I'm a black female Chicagoan poet. My first collection ended with an off-rhyme sonnet series in the voices of African-American officers, resurrecting the controversy about black poets using traditional white forms. I've been accused of degrading the sonnet with black, anti-war propaganda: and of not being black enough!

Some say poetry+politics=propaganda. That blackpoet+sonnet=sellout. I do hope your 'propaganda' sells out, continuing the long tradition of both political poetry and black poets engaging with white forms. It's literary skill that counts: always ask yourself, am I poet enough?

FROM AFRICA SINGING

Dear Patience, I write from the tradition of non-European poetry that celebrates the voice of the people, the orality of literature, spoken word, yet sometimes the struggle shrinks to a clenched fist in a European cage: a sonnet. My sonnet for Phillis Wheatley, the first Black woman to be published in America, has a 4/4 beat, internal rhyme. Did *she* write sonnets?

If she did they weren't published. Frozen in the headlights of the heroic couplet, she didn't feature in a recent dialogic sonnet sequence. A shame! Hi-5 for using the sonnet to highlight her fame and subverting it back to its roots. How many poets think 'little song' when they think 'sonnet'?

BLOOD LETTERS

'RUBY THE HYPODERMIC DJ'

after Thom Gunn

We watch through tinted shades as
Ruby begins. The boy has

picked a lyrical armband
for his lush desert island:

'While My Guitar Gently Weeps'.
Ruby chooses black ink, drops

her fine, electric needle
onto, into his clear pale

vinyl. His skin sings crimson.
He hears pain, an endorphin

buzz, the sound of the lyric
translating into bold, black.

. . . Now it's done, he pays Ruby
with crisp, clean notes. Beneath the

bandage, each wound bleeds a tone
deeper. Now he's Number One.

R.A.P.
for Carl St Hill

The last song you sang was a love song
that took your whole life to write
and the room crammed with home grown men
cried like they were shedding blood
ink on love letters
as your minor chords cast their spell.

This was the gospel
according to St Hill, the song you sang
at your own funeral *Let us*
pray as if performing last rites
on your own flesh, blood,
your soul inspiring men

and boys to men.
This was the spell
stirred your blood
brothers to battle using
Eminem-feminine rhymes, write
rap in the air in capital letters.

You should have had letters
after your name, Carl. *Amen.*
I hear your rhythms as I write
R.A.P. but how do you spell
septicaemia and how do I sing
knowing poison blocked your blood

stream of conscious lyrics, blood?
You wore letters
instead, NIKE, FUBU, made them sing
out loud, the showman, shaman
of sound who could dispel
the blues and still retain the copyright

of rhythm. Rewind. I must rewrite
these lyrics in your spirit so the beat pumps blood,
my heart jumps up when I thumbs up your spell
to set us free from the ghettos of grief, let us
break those fetters, dismantle the . . . damn! You're the man
made my tears flow like a flood of lyrical slang.

OSMOSIS

Nurse says I'll soon be well. *Read!*
It's the mind that makes the body rich.

The Complete Works. My kidneys have failed,
nurse says. I'll soon be well? Red

is all I see, the roller-coaster of blood
black words dissolving in bleach.

Nurse says I'll soon be well read.
''Tis the mind that makes the body rich.'

THERE WAS AN OLD WOMAN WHO LIVED IN A SHOE

1

There was an old shoe, a lace-up, leather,
cracked by ambition, twisted by weather.
Black as a beetle dissected and bled.
Worn by the woman whose hair was dark red.

There was an old shoe that somebody buried
with a broken brown bottle for luck when they married.
Under the floorboards they laid down their roots.
The shoe gave birth to a pair of glass boots.

There was an old shoe, a laced-up space . . .
black leather walls draped with black leather lace,
black leather floorboards, a black leather shrine
where she knelt down to pray for a word, for a line.

There was an 'old' woman, thirty years old
whose hair was the colour of antique gold.
She lived all her life in ambition's embrace.
You could almost decipher the lines on her face.

There was an old woman who lived in a *Sh!*
The twins are asleep. She was writing for two.
She prayed for red wine inspiration. She drank.
As her liver got bigger, the tiny room shrank.

There was an old bottle that met an old shoe.
She said, *I dare you* and he said, *I do.*
She said, *You're broken* and he said, *You're thin
as a rag.* She had bottle: he put the boot in.

A boot in her brain, and it grew and it grew
till the big black glass boot split into two.
Right brain, left brain, needle and thread,
they kicked and they danced themselves out of her head.

2

There was an old woman who lived in her head
with black glass walls and a black glass bed
and a fibreglass lamp that went red, that went black,
that went red. On her scalp was a hairline crack,

a tiny thin line you could barely decode,
another, another, another. They flowed
like fine-lettered stitches, like intricate lace,
a row of black letters, a row of white space.

Her head got bigger, a balloon made of glass,
the black glassy walls became spider's web scars,
the floorboards groaned as if heavy with flood
till they smashed. And the red wine turned into blood.

They split her head open. They opened her head
like a book. Stitched her quiet with black leather thread.
She cried out in splinters, her tears bottle brown.
They took out the boots, stitched her up, held her down.

There was a glass box like an intricate mind
where the delicate pair of glass boots were enshrined.
She looks through the glass at each side of her soul.
She's writing but feels like she's shovelling coal.

There was an old woman: there was an old shoe.
She lived like a foot till the sole was worn through.
There was an old shoe and a narrative thread.
Her words are alive, and her story's undead.

3

There was an old shoe with a stiff leather tongue.
There was an old woman, thirty years young.
There was a brown bottle, empty and broken,
a pair of glass boots in a box they can't open.

There was an old woman who lived in a shoe.
Some of it, none of it, all of it's true.
She died alcoholic, she died in her bed,
she died when they severed the boots from her head.

STEP

into my shoes, Imelda, said the dead queen
so I set my foot in her glass coffin,
glimpsed a powdered, rouged, mascaraed premonition
of her daughter, rigid with my Cox's poison.

The queen and I were lovers. We told no one.
She died in childbed. Every day I'm broken
to sense her killer mocking my reflection.
The mirror never lies. Neither does passion.

I'm granite cold during my confession.
They call me witch, harlot, slave to fashion
and sentence me to dance in wrought-iron
shoes hell-hot from the oven. So I step

into my deathbed, lined with scarlet satin,
studded with broken glass, next to my queen.

IN INVISIBLE INK

Imagine the tip of my tongue's a full
Needle and your back's my canvas.

I'll tattoo you a secret if you promise
Never to read it aloud, break the spell
Vibrating its delicate, intimate Braille.
It'll remain laced in your skin. Even fierce
Sunlight won't betray my lemon juice.
In less than a fortnight the scar will heal
But we'll have words, you'll set fire to my love
Letter by letter and I'll imagine somebody
Else, touch-typing the keyboard of your spine,

Imagine our secret smouldering skin and bone.
No. Don't say a word. My blind eye
Knows how to head my tongue, how to forgive.

WHAT'S BLACK AND WHITE AND RED ALL OVER?

A newspaper
delivered to a hotel room
on a silver tray
in a hotel where the head chef's
a tall black man with a bold face,
wearing a toque blanche,
stir-frying strips of marinated zebra
in a king-size wok,
the prices on the menu
inflating like the number
of columns in the national newspaper
where the news is divided
into plots but there's not enough
land to bury the dead
from AIDS – a white man's disease
the public are told; or women
writing a monthly column
in their own blood
because newspaper
is ten times cheaper
than tampons; or literacy
withering on a makeshift bed,
too ill to attend a school
that has no teachers,
so fewer can read
but everyone gets the message.

NOT THE ONE THEY READ TO TELL MY FORTUNE

Unnatural, they claimed, predicting drought,
flood, infertility, twins, orgy, famine.
My left hand gagged behind my back, I wrote
I am unclean, unfeminine
a hundred times in someone else's hand.
They did their worst
to realign my fate, my heart, my head.
Hold out your hand. Six of the best.

My brainchildren multiplied like fungus.
Cracked china dolls, I named each one of them
after old scars. My right hand has five fingers
and a withered thumb
which proved unlucky for some.

LINES

He snorts words joined at the hip, sentences whole,
       he snorts the pure white space between the lines,
titles, headlines and quotes: 'blood will have blood';
       the underbelly, the meaningful pause of subtext,
poetry because it looks like lists
but means more than it says, which makes him high,
and lists.   WINDOLENE   *   1.06
               TOMATO PUREE   0.26

He prefers long words in other languages,
Das Aufmerksamkeitsdefizitsyndrom;
to medium, hyperlexia, autism;
and short, OCD, ADD,
written in illegible handwriting;
but lists,   MR MUSCLE   *   1.15
       because when he cannot read he likes to clean
are his favourite, TINNED TOMATOES   0.45
               TINNED TOMATOES   0.45

         Chopped Tomatoes
         (70%), Tomato
         Juice, Citric Acid.

         Energy: 93kJ/22kcal
         Protein: 1.1g
         Carbohydrate: 3.5g
         Fat: 0.4g

Each night he'll watch his favourite film because
ALL WORK AND NO PLAY MAKES JACK A DULL BOY
All work.
       And no play.
              Makes Jack a dull boy.
All work and no . . . in Rich Tomato Juice
Best Before End Dec 2007.

'Thou shalt not kill.' He had a father once,
impossible to read, all adjectives
and nouns. No verbs. *The best school in the country*
and *Bitter disappointment*. Life is simple:
a shopping list, a slim volume of verse,
Mr Muscle loves the jobs you hate
and a video. *He* made it complicated,
Our Father. You were not allowed to be,
you had to be a proper noun. A Doctor,
a Lawyer, a Director. Father spoke
a different tongue. In spite of all his learning
he wrote nothing down and died intestate
leaving behind a library of hardbacks
no one else wanted. Better than cocaine
the hit of a well-turned line, line after line
singing off the page, each repetition
of rhythm, rhyme, each reading, each re-reading
bringing him closer to God. Till he *was* God.
He only said it once, but when he said it
they locked him up refusing him the Bible,
the Complete Works of Shakespeare, and they asked him
and asked him when he'd edited his father
out of the picture, where he'd done it, how.

This is how. He sentenced him in black.

He made him a blank page. He made him blanch.

Made him confess his sins in black and white.

He cut his sentence short. He made him write

his will and then he burnt the words he wrote.

He made him learn the words he burnt, by rote.

With an adjective and noun, he made him red.

Best Before End. Impossible to read.

THE EXCHANGE

INT. RESTAURANT – 8.06 p.m.

His tongue speaks brandy but his voice is hoarse.
Catches her eye, reverts from man to beast.
Her choker feeds on candlelight, its beads
are sweat. He struggles to pronounce the hors

d'oeuvres which arrive pulsating, rare.
They eat each other's hearts, a Roman feast
of Russian dolls. Then exchange the ghost
of a smile as she strips her wedding finger bare.

INT. BUS (MOVING) – 6.08 p.m.

A man stumbles upon the step, eyes bloodshot,
clutched to his chest an anarchy of blood

burning a black hole in his off-white shirt.
Only a lover's supplication would

prize open his locked hands, expose his guilt.
A severed finger, the bright stench of gold.

VICIOUS CIRCLE

VICIOUS CIRCLE

1

A basement bar. Black-and-white.
I'm at the bar on a barstool. The soundtrack,
my psychopath husband stuttering in the dark.
A ring-studded hand offers me a light.
I politely decline. This is my married lot,
dying to inhale, look back,
smile. But petrified. I'm half sick
of shadows and the stutter of gunshot.

Some dream they're being chased by death,
the action-adventure, double shot of adrenaline.
I'm freeze-framed, double whisky on ice.
'Cause I married a madman with bad breath
and I'm manacled like Lana Turner in
'The Postman Always Rings Twice'.

2

The postman always rings twice.
The bell penetrates my dream noir
like *Time! Last orders at the bar.*
I roll over to empty white space,
my husband's drunken promise
reverberating like a hangover.
I'll kill Him. His associate, my lover.
Doorbell again. My eyes

burn with daylight. White silk dressing gown.
Hall reeking of Calvados and Vim.
Recorded delivery. I've got the shakes
as I scrawl my name on the dotted line.
A brown envelope. It's from Him.
My head aches.

3

My head aches
as my body's confessing,
opening the letter like the slow undressing
of a lover anticipating sex
in the devil's triangle. It takes
five minutes to savour, like French kissing.
Both of us are trespassing.
I don't notice the spelling mistakes.

He never rings. He's committing
what adults do, on Conqueror paper,
tracing the intricate curves of my name.
I light a Marlboro, imagine His hand writing
then set fire to His signature,
my shame.

4

My shame
is an embryo kicking,
but I can't, won't stop sucking
on the same flame.
Coughing up phlegm.
My unborn child's chain smoking
behind the bike shed. I'm choking
the umbilical chain.

No. I won't give birth
to a lie. When I inspire
I breathe His dynamite.
If smoking kills, then death
becomes me. No smoke without fire,
no fire without a light.

5

No fire without a light,
I chuckle on our third rendezvous,
first time I've laughed in months. He laughs too.
I love His laugh, His whole body shakes with it,
His huge sinewy body. We both flirt.
We share the same bawdy sense of humour.
Come on, He says, spinning me onto the dance floor,
I want to see what's under your little black circle skirt.

Later, we watch the needle drop onto the vinyl.
Marry me, He says, lighting a Marlboro. I freeze.
Watching His mind's grey-green eye in slow-mo,
the seductive, covetous eye of a criminal.
I'm shaking my head but my eyes say, *Yes*.
Four months two weeks ago.

6

Four months two weeks ago
we conceived the plan. I wonder do I love Him
more than I hate my husband? Are they the same,
love and hate, love-hate my Siamese embryo?
Will there be stretchmarks on my ego?
Will I still love Him when I bear His name?
My body screams 'we're running out of time'
so why His moral vertigo?

I'll do it myself. Shoot him with his own gun.
There's no love lost. I'll have the last laugh.
How many times can you force your wife?
No faith in my lover, no cash to hire a hitman,
no way out. Let them sentence me to death,
to life.

7

To life!
We clink glasses. The bubbles sting my tongue.
But is it worth living? I snap. *I was wrong*
to trust you. This delay's beyond belief.
Is there someone else? Perhaps you've fallen in love
with him! He calls the child 'our son',
it turns my stomach. I'm crying now. *How long*
must I endure this? He laughs a brittle laugh.

Three hours. I'm killing him tonight.
You seem shocked. Thought you'd be overjoyed.
Perhaps you'd like to kiss him goodbye.
He forces the glass to my lips, *Go on, kiss the cunt.*
I splutter and choke. Appalled. Petrified.
For a split second I see my husband's bloodshot eye.

8

For a split second I see my husband's bloodshot eye,
my future spouse. I drop the champagne glass.
He reaches for my hand. *I'm sorry*, He says.
Slowly I face Him. He squeezes my hand. I sigh.
The light can play tricks on the mind but the body
feels light as heat. He strokes my face.
I've lost the power of speech so kiss
words into His mouth. In reply

His tongue traces the contour of my lips
like a paintbrush, teasing body and mind.
He pushes it inside,
kissing my mouth like a total eclipse.
Our lips are sealed, our fates are intertwined,
our tongues are tied.

9

Our tongues are tied,
hers and mine, linked like the iron
grey signature on a death warrant,
the perfect initials proving suicide.
I'll kill him. To make her my bride?
To save her from his psycho tyranny?
I wish. Deliver us from irony.
Four months two weeks ago, I lied.

I'll kill him. Not for the smell of red roses,
the delicate bouquet of pre-war vintage.
I prefer the stench of cash to a millionairess,
hard cash that squats in suitcases.
I've been paid to hate him, a man in my own image.
Wish I loved her more, 'hated' him less.

10

Wish I loved her more, hated him less.
I can read her body, mind but I'm two-faced,
fit my huge hands round her wasp waist.
She's a devil in a bullet-proof dress.
I could kill for love. I'm killing for The Boss.
Two motives yet I'm in two minds. We share a past
and he's Family. It leaves a bad taste.
I'll wear his death like an albatross.

And what if the kid's his? No. Her sand's
shifting fast. It's now or never. I'll ring her
in an hour's time. We both have an alibi.
I built him up from nothing with my bare hands,
I'll kill him with the flick of my forefinger.
He's worse than nothing but who am I?

11

He's worse than nothing but who am I
to film his death through the muzzle of a gun
in a basement bar? Bloodshot monochrome.
Seeing fear, betrayal flash through the lens of his eye.
I betray nothing. He stutters blood. Bleeds dry.
No one else shoots but words speak louder than actions,
silence louder than accusations.
As I leave I notice the pockmarked walls, the sly

wink from the barmaid. I let the phone ring twice
then hang up. Mum'll swear on my father's life
I was at hers for dinner. None of the mob'll squeak.
Cold meat and two veg. A stiff, a full suitcase
and the love of a good woman. I'm safe if
only money can speak.

12

Only money can speak
and it spits the staccato rage of a fanatic
who makes war, torture and death poetic.
Men desire it more than sex.
It's the new religion, the six six six,
history repeating its histrionics.
I open the suitcase wide as a good fuck.
Its breath stinks.

Love has been interrupted,
silenced with cash, debased to lust.
Tomorrow I'll buy the ring
and she'll belong to me. Dearly beloved.
For richer for poorer. Dust to dust.
Without her I'm nothing.

13

Without her I'm nothing.
I lie down, feel her hands unbuttoning my shirt,
releasing the thick black rope of my belt.
I can hear her breathing.
Feel each breath on my skin, her lips mouthing
my name over and over. She licks salt, sweat,
whisky from my lips. We link tongues, suck, bite
as she strips each layer of clothing.

Knocking to wake the dead.
A premonition, the bite of metal round my wrists.
But my hands continue unzipping her little black number,
unfastening the clasp of her bra. And she's beside
herself. The noise fades. She's unclenching her fists.
I'm inside her.

14

I'm inside her
recurring dream, knocking back doubles.
His machine-gun laughter sprays the pockmarked walls.
I watch her drinking whisky on the rocks at the bar.
She takes out a Marlboro. I offer my lighter,
anything to see her face. She blinks, smiles
with her eyes, barely moving her muscles.
She declines. But her smile inches wider.

The laughter dies like a fake alibi.
He's walking towards me. I can hear her crying.
I struggle to wake up but I can't quite.
The last thing I see before I die,
the vicious gaze of his gun's eye in
a basement bar. Black. And white.

NOTES

Grey Area: A South African term referring to an area where black and white people lived at the end of the apartheid era. In Britain it refers to a region in which unemployment is relatively high.

Shooting 'Ufo Woman': 'Ufo Woman', a sci-fi poem in *Transformatrix*, was made into a short film for Channel Four's *Litpop* series in 1998.

The London Eye: A SKIN .Beat™ is a type of Swatch which came out in 2002.

Comedown: Heaven is a gay nightclub in central London.

North(west)ern: The music celebrated is Northern Soul, rare '60s and early '70s dance music especially popular in the northwest of England. It's affectionately known as 'Northern'.

Yore Just My Type: Gaydar is an online gay dating agency.

Skins: 'I passed' is short for 'I passed for white' i.e. I was mistakenly accepted as a white person.

Josephine Baker Finds Herself: 'La Garçonne' was a term used to describe a sexually liberated woman in the 1920s.

In Joy and Woe, Henry Howard, Earl of Surrey: Title from sonnet, 'Alas! so all Things now do Hold their Peace'.

Two Loves I Have, William Shakespeare: Title from sonnet 144, 'Two loves I have, of comfort and despair'; the phrase 'dressing old words new' from sonnet 76, 'Why is my verse so barren of new pride'.

A Crowne of Sonnets, Lady Mary Wroth: Title from 'A Crowne of Sonnets dedicated to Love' at the end of *Pamphilia to*

Amphilanthus; 'Look in thy heart, and write' from the opening sonnet of the sequence *Astrophel and Stella* by Sir Philip Sydney, her uncle.

My Light Is Spent, John Milton: Title from sonnet 'When I consider how my light is spent' in which 'patience' responds to his question in the sestet, subliminally giving me the concept for *Problem Pages*; 'imbreed and cherish in a great people the seeds of virtue and public civility' appears in Milton's essay *The Reason of Church-government Urg'd Against Prelaty.*

Queen of Shadows, Charlotte Smith: Title from sonnet 'To Fancy'.

Scorn Not the Sonnet, William Wordsworth: Title from 'Scorn not the sonnet; critic, you have frown'd'; 'He and my beloved sister are the two beings to whom my intellect is most indebted' appears in a letter, 1832. 'He' is Samuel Taylor Coleridge; Wordsworth admired Milton's sonnets for their 'simplicity and unity of object and aim' in a letter to his brother John, November 1802; Coleridge criticises Wordsworth's 'habit' of writing 'such a multitude of small poems' in a letter to Thomas Poole, 14 October 1803.

O for Ten Years . . . , John Keats: Title from 'Sleep and Poetry'.

Not Death, but Love, Elizabeth Barrett Browning: Title from sonnet 1 of the sequence, *Sonnets from the Portuguese*; 'the "mingled yarn" is black and white' appears in a letter to a friend.

Send My Roots Rain, Gerard Manley Hopkins: Title from sonnet, 'Thou art indeed just, Lord, if I contend'; 'No doubt my poetry errs on the side of oddness . . . design, pattern or what I call *inscape* is what I above all aim at in poetry' appears in a letter to Robert Bridges, 1879.

Knew White Speech, Gwendolyn Brooks: Title from sonnet 1 of the sequence *Gay Chaps at the Bar.*

From Africa Singing, June Jordan: Title from sonnet 'Something Like A Sonnet for Phillis Miracle Wheatley', the subtitle of her essay, 'The Difficult Miracle of Black Poetry in America'.

R.A.P.: 'Blood' is a slang word for a close friend.

REBEL WITHOUT APPLAUSE
Lemn Sissay

"Lemn Sissay has success written on his forehead."
Guardian

Lemn Sissay's poems are laid into the streets of downtown
Manchester, feature on the side of a public house in the
same city and have been emblazoned on a central London
bus route. He has been commissioned to write poetry,
documentaries and plays for Radio 1 and Radio 4, as
well as being involved in television in the roles of writing,
performing and presenting. He also features on the
Leftfield album, *Leftism*.

"The product of an imagination that is rare, passionate,
committed, occasionally distraught, funny and tender."
Straight No Chaser

ISBN 978 1 84195 001 3

£9.99

www.canongate.tv

MORNING BREAKS IN THE ELEVATOR
Lemn Sissay

"A lyrical genius." *The Voice*

This is a twist of Lemn. There is no smokescreen, no
flim-flam or slim-slam. Between this collection and his
previous one the BBC has done a documentary about his
life, he's presented *Jazz606* on BBC2, written plays and
read his work all around the world but he has still found
Gold from the Stone. This is the reason his *Morning Breaks
in the Elevator*. Read on.

"Fierce, funny, serious, satirical, streetwise and tender."
Big Issue

ISBN 978 086241 838 0

£9.99

www.canongate.tv

TRANSFORMATRIX
Patience Agbabi

TRANSFORMATRIX
PATIENCE AGBABI

"A wonderful subversion of cultural myths." *Time Out*

From Hamburg to Jo'Burg, Oslo to Soho, Patience Agbabi
follows her critically acclaimed debut collection, *R.A.W.*,
with *Transformatrix*, an exploration of women, travel and
metamorphosis. Inspired by '90s poetry, '80s rap and '70s
disco, *Transformatrix* is a celebration of literary form and
constitutes a very potent and telling commentary on the
realities of modern Britain. It is also a self-portrait of a poet
whose honesty, intelligence and wit pack a punch, draw a
smile and warm your heart – all at once.

"A rising star." *Observer*

"Patience Agbabi is only more proof that great performance
poetry can bring to the page that raw, wicked stuff that has
brought British poetry back to life." Benjamin Zephaniah

ISBN 978 08624 1 941 7

£9.99

www.canongate.tv